Light Codes: The Art of Stillness

Mal Stevens

Light Codes: The Art of Stillness

Meditation for those who came from the stars — and are ready to return to their truth

Copyright © 2025 Mal Stevens

All rights reserved. No part of this book may be reproduced or transmitted in any form or by any means, electronic or mechanical, including information storage and retrieval systems, without prior written permission from the author, except for brief quotations used in reviews.

This book is a work of fiction. Names, characters, places, and events are products of the author's imagination or are used fictitiously. Any resemblance to real persons, living or dead, or actual events is purely coincidental.

Disclaimer

This book is for informational and educational purposes only and is not intended as a substitute for professional medical advice, diagnosis, or treatment. The author is not a medical doctor and assumes no responsibility for outcomes resulting from the use of the information or practices contained herein.

ISBN 978-0-6456803-9-3 (Paperback)
ISBN 978-1-7644628-0-8 (eBook)

www.malstevens.com.au

Dedications

For **Marinda, Aimee, Steven, and Lily**, my daily reminder of all that is good in this world. I Love You X

~*~

For **Marinda and Silla** —
Star-Born, Soul-Breathed, and Entirely One of a Kind

~*~

"To know yourself as the Being underneath the thinker, the stillness underneath the mental noise, the love and joy underneath the pain, is freedom, salvation, enlightenment."
— Eckhart Tolle, The Power of Now

in silentio invenies te ipsum

Table of Contents

Preface 2

Introduction 4

Cosmic Overload & the Quiet Within 7

Meditation — The Art of Returning Home 10

The Energy of Stillness 13

When Meditation Doesn't Seem to Work 17

The Light Body and Galactic Connection 23

The Healing Frequencies of Meditation 27

The Benefits of Meditation 32

How Meditation Transforms the Physical Body 34

Awakening the Galactic Heart 37

Meditation as a Portal to Higher Consciousness 39

Meditation and Belief — Beyond Religion 44

The Practice of Presence 48

Creating Your Daily Meditation Practice 53

The Healing Frequencies of Meditation 59

The Light Body and Galactic Connection 66

The Practice of Galactic Meditation 73

Activating the Crystalline DNA 80

The Starseed Remembering 86

Anchoring Light on Earth 91

The Golden Heart and the Frequency of Love 98

The Celestial Breath 104

The Galactic Mind and Higher Consciousness 110

The Path of Light Integration	116
The Light Codes of Creation	123
The Ascension of Everyday Life	128
The Return to the Stars	134
Practices for Returning Home to the Stars	140
The Light Remains	149
Author's Note - From My Heart to Yours	151

There's no single "right" amount of time - it depends on intention and consistency.

But here's what both modern neuroscience and ancient practice suggest:

Purpose	Optimum Duration	Frequency	Why it Works
Daily grounding / stress relief	10–15 minutes	1–2 times daily	Calms the nervous system, reduces cortisol, trains focus.
Deep emotional release / inner journey	20–30 minutes	A few times a week	Allows entry into theta brainwaves (deep healing state).
Spiritual growth / energy attunement	15–25 minutes	Daily	Enhances energy flow, awareness, and intuitive expansion.

The "Light Codes: The Art of Stillness" theme is perfect as it aligns beautifully with how long the mind needs to shift from beta (thinking) to alpha/theta (healing and creativity).

Consistency matters more than duration — 15 minutes daily is far more transformative than one long weekly session.

"You have never been lost. You were simply waiting to remember."

Preface

There is a language older than words—
the quiet pulse of the stars,
the breath between heartbeats,
the stillness that remembers where we came from.

You are a being of light, woven from the same essence as the constellations. Yet life on Earth can make even the brightest soul forget. The noise, the haste, the heaviness of modern living veil the truth that peace has never been lost—it has only been forgotten beneath layers of thought.

This little book is your map home.

Within these pages, you will find a simple, sacred practice—fifteen minutes a day that can open gateways of calm, clarity, and remembrance. Through meditation and the gentle currents of star being energy healing, you will learn to listen again—to your breath, to your energy, to the whisper of the stars within you.

Meditation transformed my life completely. It softened my fears, rekindled my intuition, and restored the quiet joy that waits beneath every storm. In stillness, I found the Universe breathing with me—guiding, healing, reminding.

You don't need a mountaintop or a monastery. You only need this moment, and a willingness to pause.

Meditation is not about becoming something new—it is about remembering who you already are.

It is natural, loving, and profoundly empowering. It is the pathway back to your own starlight.

May these words and practices be your lantern.

May you rediscover your own rhythm of peace.

And may your light ripple out into the world — one breath, one heartbeat, one star at a time.

With infinite love and luminous blessings,
Mal Stevens x

"In the stillness between breaths, the stars begin to whisper who you've always been."

Introduction

This little book is not only about learning how to meditate—it is about remembering how to be.

It is about quieting the noise long enough to hear your soul again.

You will, of course, learn the practical steps: how to meditate, when, where, and why.

But far more importantly, you will discover what meditation truly is—a sacred return to presence. A remembering of your connection to the greater whole: to the Earth beneath you, the breath within you, and the stars above that are made of the same light as your spirit.

When practiced with intention, meditation reshapes everything it touches.

It calms the mind, softens the heart, and reawakens the energy systems that nourish the body.

It can improve your physical health, deepen emotional balance, awaken intuition, and strengthen your connection to the Source of all life—whatever name you give it: Universe, Spirit, God, or simply Love.

Through stillness, people have found healing for anxiety and fear.

They have released old grief, rebalanced their hormones, soothed inflammation, restored focus, and rediscovered the joy they thought they'd lost.

Meditation is not magic—it is simply *you* returning to your natural state of harmony.

Many believe meditation is about emptying the mind or sitting perfectly still in the lotus pose, trying not to think. But true meditation is not about escaping thought; it is about observing it.

It is learning to watch the endless dance of the mind with compassion, until—like dust settling on sunlight—everything becomes clear again.

In these pages, you will come to understand the inner workings of your mind and energy field. You'll see how your thoughts shape your health, how your emotions guide your vibration, and how your spirit communicates through sensation and silence.

You will learn gentle, practical ways to still the "monkey mind," release tension, and open the sacred channels of peace, joy, and creativity that have always lived within you.

Each breath you take during meditation is a declaration of sovereignty.

A choice to step out of the noise and come home to yourself.

With time, you will find that the chatter fades, your intuition deepens, your energy brightens, and your heart expands to meet the rhythm of the stars once more.

It may sound miraculous, but it is not too good to be true. It is your birthright.

For too long, the simple truth has been hidden in plain sight—that stillness is the most powerful medicine we possess.

Now, both science and spirit agree: the light you seek has always been within you.

And all it asks for… is fifteen minutes a day.

"The stars have never been far away — they've only been waiting for your eyes to close and remember."

Cosmic Overload & the Quiet Within

In recent years, a growing body of clinical research has confirmed what seers and star-beings have known for ages: our modern lives carry a heavy load—not just of busyness, but of energetic turbulence, unprocessed emotion, and silent disconnection from the deeper currents of existence.

Meditation is no longer considered an obscure Eastern ritual—it has entered mainstream consciousness as a natural, simple and profoundly powerful healing practice.

As you read this book, you may already sense the call of something greater—a longing not just to relax, but to awaken. Whether you are new to meditation or have dipped your toes into its still waters before, this guide will help you step deeper: understanding what meditation truly is, how it can transform your entire life, and how you can easily make it a daily ritual of remembrance.

If you are committed to meditating properly, the first step is to recognise *why* it matters—not only for your physical or mental health, but for your spiritual alignment as a being of light and connection. Many people begin meditation simply because they wish to ease their overload, quiet their minds, or shift an inner frequency (personal growth).

But did you know that through regular meditation you can dramatically improve your well-being by clearing the subtle burdens your body and energy field carry? Research shows that meditation can reduce inflammation, modulate deep brain regions tied to emotional regulation and memory, and support the healing of your multi-dimensional self.

Our contemporary Western lives often carry a relentless sense of overload—and not just physical tasks. We juggle work, family, homes, social obligations—and underneath that, many of us bear the echoes of past trauma, unspoken fears, energetic imprints from another lifetime. In short: we carry layers of accumulated burden.

In the traditional "fight-or-flight" model the body cycles between beacon alerts and rest; but what we now face is often a state of "still threat"—not a lion in the bush, but a memory, an expectation, a ripple of energy signalling "You must act." The body responds. The mind responds. And yet no primal action is required—and still the energy circulates. We stay in high-alert modes much longer than nature ever intended.

Here's where star being energy healing and the meditation we'll practice together come in. Star being energy healing invites you to release not only the surface symptoms of overload, but the unseen: energetic blockages, subconscious beliefs, past-life echoes, the starlit imprint of your being that's been dimmed in earthly time.

Because when we dwell too long in the state of perceived urgency—when we live perpetually on the edge of our survival systems—our body cannot function as it was designed to: digestion slows, immunity weakens, creativity dulls, clarity clouds, sense of purpose dims. Research shows many of our common health issues—from anxiety and skin conditions to chronic fatigue and digestive disorders—are now linked with this prolonged state of overload.

But here's the luminous truth: You are not broken. You are recalibrating.

Your nervous system, your energy body, the star code within you—they all remember peace. Through meditation you are invited into stillness. You are called into presence.

You are returning to your own frequency of light.

Soon in this book you'll find a practical list of gentle daily practices that will significantly ease your overload and awaken your starlight.

You don't need to climb a mountain. You just need a breath, a quiet space, and fifteen minutes a day to reclaim the truth of your light-body.

"Every breath of stillness is a galaxy unfolding within you."

Meditation — The Art of Returning Home

When many people imagine meditation, they picture someone sitting cross-legged in perfect stillness, perhaps on a mountain peak, eyes closed, mind emptied of all thought. While that image holds beauty, it also carries a quiet myth — that meditation is something difficult, disciplined, or reserved for spiritual masters.

In truth, meditation is far more natural than that. It is not an act of twisting the body into impossible shapes, nor of forcing the mind into silence. It is simply the art of coming home to yourself.

Meditation can happen anywhere — in your chair, your garden, even in the quiet pause between sips of tea. It is not about escaping life but entering it more fully. You do not need to still every thought; you only need to observe them with kindness until their noise softens and your inner voice begins to rise.

For many, the greatest barrier to meditation is the belief that it's difficult, time-consuming, or boring. But once you experience its still magic, you realise it's none of those things. Meditation is ease itself — gentle, enjoyable, and endlessly rewarding. It opens the pathways of light and awareness that already flow within you.

In this age of awakening, meditation has evolved beyond tradition. It now embraces both the ancient and the cosmic — breathwork, sound frequency, galactic alignment, energy healing, and star consciousness. Each approach is a doorway. The key is to find the one that feels most alive for you.

No two souls meditate in exactly the same way, because no two souls are vibrating at the same frequency. Some may find peace in quiet breathing, others through guided journeys, energy attunements, or visualising the golden grid of starlight connecting all things.

The most powerful meditation practice is always the one that feels like home.

It's the one that fits gracefully into your life — not forced, but flowing.

When you discover that, meditation ceases to be a chore and becomes a joy, a moment you look forward to — your daily reunion with the light within.

So, let go of what you think meditation should look like.

Instead, allow it to become what your soul most needs.

Because meditation is not about perfect stillness.

It's about perfect presence.

And that, dear star being, is where you will rediscover yourself.

"You were made of stardust so you could remember how to shine."

The Energy of Stillness

When you begin to meditate, you are not just calming your mind — you are tuning your entire energetic field to a higher vibration.

Stillness is not empty. It is *alive*. It hums with intelligence, light, and creation itself.

Within every moment of stillness, energy moves.

Beneath the hush of your thoughts, your energy body — your light body — begins to expand, harmonise, and remember its original frequency.

This is the quiet miracle of meditation: while the mind believes it is doing nothing, the soul is rebuilding worlds within.

Through star being energy healing, this understanding deepens.

Star being energy healing meditation teaches that we are more than physical beings — we are multidimensional souls, layered in subtle energy bodies that record every experience, thought, and emotion. These layers can become heavy or distorted through fear, stress, or trauma.

But in stillness, we reconnect with Source — the higher light that realigns and purifies those layers, restoring balance and flow.

Each breath you take in meditation becomes a current of energy moving through your entire being.

As you exhale, you release dense vibrations — the old stories, the tension, the inherited patterns.

As you inhale, you invite in fresh frequencies — light, peace, and cosmic remembrance.

Over time, this process re-awakens the crystalline grid of your light body — the same energy network that links you to the Earth, the stars, and every soul across the galaxies.

Meditation is, therefore, not just a mental practice but an energetic activation. It opens portals within you — to your higher self, to your guides, to the wisdom of the cosmos. You begin to sense the subtle vibrations of other realms: the gentle hum of your chakras, the golden threads of starlight connecting heart to Universe.

The more you sit in stillness, the clearer those connections become.

You may notice tingling in your hands, warmth in your chest, waves of emotion, or even visions of colour and light. These are not random sensations; they are signs of movement — your energy field remembering how to sing again.

In star being energy healing meditation, we call this process energetic recalibration.

It is how the soul heals itself — not through effort, but through allowing.

When you become still, you allow life force to flow again, to fill the places that have been empty for too long.

In that moment, you are not separate from anything.

You are the Earth breathing.

You are the stars pulsing.

You are the infinite field of creation, remembering its own perfection.

Meditation is the bridge between the human and the divine — between thought and knowing, between doing and being.

In stillness, energy becomes light.

And in that light, you remember you have never been lost, only waiting to awaken.

"When you sit in silence, the constellations rearrange themselves to spell your name."

When Meditation Doesn't Seem to Work

You've probably heard it before—

"I tried meditation, but it doesn't work for me."

Maybe you've even whispered those words yourself.

I've heard them many times across years of teaching and healing, and every time, my heart smiles gently. Because meditation always works—it just doesn't always work the same way for everyone.

Some people fall in love with meditation instantly. They crave that sacred space each day like air. They feel lighter, more at peace, more attuned to the rhythm of life.

Others struggle. Their mind resists. Their body fidgets. They decide it's "not for them."

But here's the truth, dear one: if meditation feels like it isn't working, it simply means you haven't yet found your doorway in.

The Many Pathways to Stillness

Modern research continues to confirm what the ancients and the star beings have always known: those who meditate regularly experience clearer focus, better emotional balance, improved immunity, and a deeper sense of joy and connection.

Their lives don't necessarily become free of challenges—but they learn to move through them with grace rather than resistance.

So why do some people find it effortless while others feel blocked? The answer is simple—we all receive and process energy differently.

On Earth, this is described through learning styles; in the language of spirit, it is the way your soul translates vibration into experience. Each of us has a unique way of feeling the Universe—seeing it, hearing it, or sensing it through movement and emotion.

Finding Your Soul's Learning Language

One of the simplest models for understanding this is the VARK model, developed by educator Neil Fleming. It recognises four primary learning styles (plus combinations of them):

- **Visual learners** see and imagine. They think in images and symbols. They're the dreamers, visionaries, and visualisers of the world.

- **Auditory learners** hear and speak. They connect through sound, words, rhythm, and vibration.

- **Read/Write learners** translate energy through language. They are the scribes and storytellers of the stars — those who process the Universe through words, journaling, reflection, and sacred writing. For them, the act of reading or writing becomes its own meditation, a bridge between thought and awakening.

- **Kinaesthetic (tactile) learners** feel and move. They learn through experience, through the senses and the emotions.

Each soul carries a primary mode of perception—a dominant frequency of awareness—and your best meditation style flows from that.

If You Are a Visual Soul

You'll be drawn to meditations that allow the mind's eye to open—guided visualisations, creative imagery, mandalas, starlight journeys, or colour breathing.

In your meditations, you may see geometric patterns, light beings, galaxies, or symbolic visions. This is your inner universe speaking in its native language.

If You Are an Auditory Soul

You are tuned to the harmony of sound. You may connect most deeply through mantra repetition, sacred chanting, binaural beats, or the vibration of crystal bowls.

For you, the stillness arrives not in silence, but in *resonance*. The hum of "Om," the whisper of wind, the rhythm of your own breath becomes the song of your spirit.

If You Are a Read/Write Soul

You find your stillness in words — in the quiet rhythm between thought and ink.

Your meditation may take the form of journaling, automatic writing, poetry, or even reading sacred texts that awaken remembrance.

For you, writing is meditation — each word becomes a mantra, each sentence a frequency aligning thought with higher truth.

When you write, you anchor light into form. You translate energy into language, giving the unseen a voice.

If You Are a Kinaesthetic Soul

You feel life through your body. Stillness comes through movement and embodiment—walking meditations, dance meditations, candle gazing, or the feeling of waves against your skin.

Your connection awakens through sensation and flow, through touch, through rhythm, through doing. You don't need to sit perfectly still—you need to feel perfectly alive.

There Is No Wrong Doorway

If meditation hasn't worked for you in the past, you simply entered through the wrong doorway. The Universe offers infinite ways to meet the same stillness.

When you align your meditation practice with your natural style of perception, everything changes. You no longer force silence; you fall into it.

You begin to look forward to that sacred fifteen minutes a day—because it feels like coming home.

The One Practice for Every Soul

There is one form of meditation that transcends all learning styles—Zen, or simply presence.

Zen meditation asks for nothing but this: Be here now.

No images, no sounds, no rules—only the awareness of this moment as it unfolds.

Whether you see, hear, or feel energy, the Now belongs to all of us.

When you sit in presence, you are no longer a student trying to meditate—you are the meditation itself.

The breath breathes you.

The stars move through you.

The Universe becomes aware of itself through your stillness.

And that is the true miracle.

"The light you seek in the heavens is the same light that beats in your chest."

The Light Body and Galactic Connection

As your meditation deepens, you begin to sense that what you are awakening is not just the mind — but the light body, the true architecture of your soul.

Every being of light carries a luminous field of energy that extends far beyond the physical form. It is the subtle scaffolding of consciousness, woven from frequencies of colour, sound, and sacred geometry. In star being energy healing meditation, this field is understood as a multidimensional system — a bridge between human awareness and higher realms of existence.

When you enter meditation, you activate this field.

Your light body begins to expand, to breathe, to remember.

You are not just relaxing — you are realigning with your original vibration, the signature tone of your soul before time and memory shaped it.

The stillness you create through meditation becomes the tuning fork through which your energy harmonises with the higher frequencies of the cosmos. You start to feel connected again — not just to your own body and breath, but to the planetary grid, the crystalline light of the Earth, and the great web of starlight that links all conscious beings.

Your cells respond to this reconnection.

Science now tells us that meditation alters the expression of genes related to healing, stress, and immunity. Spirit tells us this is simply your light body remembering how to sing in tune with creation. Each breath, each pause, each heartbeat sends ripples through the energetic lattice that surrounds and sustains you.

Over time, these ripples awaken star memory.

You may begin to dream in symbols of light, to feel drawn to certain constellations, to experience moments of deep knowing that seem to come from somewhere far beyond this lifetime. This is no accident. The soul remembers its origins — and meditation opens the channel for that remembrance to flow once more.

Within the star being energy healing frequencies, this process is known as soul reconnection. It is a gentle awakening — not forced but allowed. As you meditate, energy flows through your higher chakras, aligning the crown, the third eye, and the heart. You begin to communicate with your higher self, your guides, and even with the galactic families who walk beside humanity through light, not form.

You may sense them as waves of peace, as tingles across the scalp, as soft pulses of energy in the hands or chest. Sometimes you'll see them in meditation as forms of gold, blue, or white light. They come not to instruct, but to remind — to reflect back the vastness you already are.

Your light body is their language.

Through it, you remember that you are not a single human struggling on one small planet, but an eternal consciousness exploring density and light — a traveller of galaxies, here to reawaken love in material form.

This is the deeper gift of meditation: it is a meeting place between worlds. It reconnects you not only to peace and presence, but to purpose — the sacred purpose of remembering who and what you truly are.

So, when you next close your eyes, feel your breath settle, and your awareness drift into stillness, know this: you are not meditating to escape life.

You are meditating to embody your light.

You are awakening the galactic within the human.

You are weaving heaven into Earth.

You are remembering the song of your own creation.

"Even the stars pause to listen when you are still."

The Healing Frequencies of Meditation

Every moment you enter meditation; you become both the healer and the healed.

You move beyond the boundaries of the physical self and into the realm of pure vibration — the place where sound becomes light and thought becomes creation.

Healing is not something that happens to you. It is something that awakens within you.

Through stillness, you begin to remember how to harmonise your body, mind, and energy with the greater pulse of the Universe.

In the star being energy healing tradition, meditation is more than a practice — it is an activation.

Each breath becomes a frequency; each pause, a point of recalibration.

Your energy field, long dulled by noise and distraction, begins to shimmer again — soft waves of golden light moving through every cell, gently loosening the emotional debris that has settled there.

These are the healing frequencies — subtle vibrations of peace, love, and remembrance that flow through your energy bodies when you surrender into stillness.

Healing the Emotional Body

Emotions are energy in motion — currents that shape how you experience life.

Over time, unexpressed emotion can crystallise within the body as tension, fatigue, or dis-ease. But in meditation, when the mind quiets and the breath deepens, those emotions begin to rise like bubbles through water — surfacing not to harm you, but to be released.

Star being energy healing meditation recognises this as the natural purification of the emotional body.

As you meditate, you may feel warmth, tingling, or even tears — these are the frequencies of release. The old patterns dissolve, and your system begins to vibrate closer to its original tone: love.

Balancing the Chakras

Each chakra — from root to crown — is a vortex of light, a gateway of awareness that bridges the physical and the spiritual.

Meditation is one of the most direct ways to clear, align, and activate these energy centres.

- When your **Root Chakra** is calm, you feel safe and grounded upon the Earth.
- When your **Sacral Chakra** opens, creativity and joy begin to flow again.
- When your **Solar Plexus** aligns, confidence and purpose are restored.
- When your **Heart Chakra** expands, compassion replaces fear.
- When your **Throat Chakra** clears, your voice becomes a channel of truth.
- When your **Third Eye** awakens, intuition and clarity guide your steps.
- And when your **Crown Chakra** blooms, you remember your divinity — the infinite light of Source.

With every meditation, these seven suns within you begin to glow brighter, harmonising into one radiant field — the unified light of your soul.

Opening the Heart Field

The heart is the bridge between the human and the divine — the place where energy becomes love, and love becomes healing.

Meditation softens the protective layers around the heart, allowing light to flow more freely through your being.

When your heart field expands, you begin to feel connected to all life — not as an idea, but as a living truth.

You sense the pulse of the stars, the rhythm of the oceans, the hum of the Earth beneath your feet.

In that space, forgiveness blossoms naturally, compassion flows without effort, and gratitude becomes your native language.

This is where true healing occurs — not in fixing, but in remembering wholeness.

Healing Across Dimensions

Star being energy healing frequencies work across time and dimension. As you sit in meditation, you may be clearing not only this life's imprints but also energies carried through ancestral or soul lineages. You might sense the release of old vows, karmic cords, or patterns of pain that have travelled with you through lifetimes.

Each meditation becomes a bridge — connecting your present self with the timeless, infinite being that you truly are.

The light you call in doesn't just heal you; it ripples outward into your lineage, your relationships, your future timelines, and even the collective field of Earth.

You heal yourself, and by doing so, you heal worlds.

Becoming a Frequency of Light

When meditation becomes your daily rhythm, healing is no longer an occasional event — it is your natural state.

You begin to vibrate differently.

You attract peace instead of conflict, clarity instead of confusion, and love instead of fear.

Your light body stabilises, your energy field strengthens, and your heart becomes the quiet sun around which your life orbits.

This is the highest purpose of meditation — not escape, but embodiment. Not transcendence, but presence.

Through stillness, you awaken the healer within — and through your light, the Universe remembers its own wholeness.

"In the quiet, your cosmic heart begins to hum with the memory of home."

The Benefits of Meditation

Every time you enter meditation, something within you begins to heal, harmonise, and remember.

Even if you don't feel it straight away, your energy responds — gently at first, then profoundly over time.

The extent of your transformation will always mirror your devotion. A few quiet minutes may soothe the mind; a regular practice will rewire your whole being. When you give yourself at least fifteen to twenty minutes of stillness each day, the Universe responds in kind — aligning body, mind, and spirit into luminous coherence.

The Gifts You Will Begin to Notice

- A deep, almost sacred sense of calm that softens the edges of daily life.
- Clarity of thought — the noise begins to settle, and intuition starts to rise.
- A grounded confidence, born not of ego, but of knowing who you truly are.
- Lighter emotions, freer breath, and the feeling of being gently held by life.
- Restful sleep, balanced energy, and renewed vitality.

- A stronger, healthier body that seems to heal faster and flow easier.
- Greater creativity, focus, and inspiration — as if your inner universe has reawakened.

These are not coincidences; they are frequencies.

Meditation adjusts your energetic resonance, allowing you to move through the world with more peace, joy, and purpose.

"You are the sky learning to see its own stars."

How Meditation Transforms the Physical Body

Modern research continues to affirm what the mystics have long taught: meditation changes the body at a cellular level. It lowers blood pressure, steadies the heartbeat, regulates hormones, strengthens the immune system, and decreases inflammation.

In essence, meditation activates what science calls the relaxation response, and what star beings might call the light recalibration — a shift from survival into creation.

When the nervous system relaxes, your light body expands. The cells begin to communicate with higher frequencies of coherence, guiding the physical body back into balance. Many practitioners notice improvements in vision, skin tone, metabolism, and energy flow. These are not "side effects" — they are signs that your system is remembering how to function as light designed it to.

Emotional, Mental, and Spiritual Renewal

Meditation clears the fog of overthinking, releasing stored emotion and old trauma that no longer serves your evolution.

Each time you sit in stillness, you are teaching your mind to become an ally, not a master. You begin to experience life from the inside out — responding with awareness rather than reacting from fear.

Your emotional field becomes steadier. Your relationships deepen. You stop seeking validation in the external world, because you are learning to draw peace from within.

Spiritually, you begin to glow differently. The chakras align. The heart expands. Synchronicities increase. You attract people and experiences that resonate with your higher vibration. The more you meditate, the more life mirrors your inner light.

Beyond the Practice — A New Way of Being

One of the greatest gifts of meditation is that its benefits extend far beyond the cushion. The peace you cultivate in silence follows you into conversation, work, and daily motion.

You begin to walk more softly, speak more kindly, and live more consciously.

Meditation strengthens the bridge between your human self and your cosmic self — your Earth walk and your galactic memory.

It helps you become the calm in the storm, the light in the chaos, the still point in the turning world.

Those who meditate regularly often find that they:

- Laugh more easily and forgive more quickly.
- Radiate a quiet joy that draws others in.
- Rest more deeply and wake more inspired.
- Create effortlessly, because they are in flow with the Universe itself.

It is no exaggeration to say that meditation enhances every aspect of your life — from health and creativity to love and purpose.

The True Secret

The true secret of meditation is not in its complexity, but in its consistency.

When you show up for your stillness each day, the Universe meets you there.

Your mind softens, your energy expands, and your light body awakens — not through striving, but through remembering.

The more you meditate, the more you return to the truth of what you are: a being of pure consciousness, radiant with starlight, living the miracle of presence on Earth.

"You are not beneath the stars — you are among them, disguised as light in human form."

Awakening the Galactic Heart

The heart is the most powerful transmitter in your energy system. It bridges the human and the infinite — the soft pulse within your chest that echoes the rhythm of the Universe itself. When you meditate, you are not only calming your mind; you are activating the Galactic Heart, the radiant centre through which divine love flows.

This awakening is both intimate and cosmic. It begins quietly — with a single breath, a single moment of stillness. Then, like a star remembering its own light, your heart field expands beyond the body, connecting with the crystalline grid of consciousness that links every being, planet, and star.

The star being energy healing frequencies work through this field. Each time you enter meditation, subtle waves of light ripple through your chakras, dissolving old patterns of fear, grief, and separation. You may feel warmth in your chest or tears that rise for no reason — this is your heart remembering how to feel the Universe again.

As this frequency deepens, you begin to sense that love is not an emotion — it is a state of being. It is the original vibration of Source. The more you dwell within it, the more your consciousness expands, and the more easily you can feel your connection to all life — the stars, the Earth, and the souls who journey beside you.

When the Galactic Heart awakens, compassion becomes effortless. You no longer seek love; you radiate it. You begin to attract synchronicities that align with your higher path — relationships that reflect truth, opportunities that nourish growth, and guidance that flows like starlight into your awareness.

Meditation is the key that opens this temple within.

Each breath is a prayer, each silence a transmission.

Through the Galactic Heart, you learn to live as love incarnate — not separate from the Universe, but as the heartbeat of it.

When you rest in this space, you are home.

And in that home, the stars sing your name.

"Each breath carries the wisdom of a thousand constellations."

Meditation as a Portal to Higher Consciousness

Meditation is far more than a practice of stillness — it is a portal.

A bridge between the physical and the infinite, between the self you know and the vast intelligence that watches through your eyes.

When you meditate, you begin to shift from human perception into galactic awareness.

This is not about worship, nor about following belief — it is about remembering your multidimensional nature.

You are not a body seeking light; you are light exploring embodiment.

The Gateway Within

The Universe is not "out there" — it unfolds within you.

Each time you close your eyes and turn inward, you are entering the living architecture of the cosmos.

The stars you gaze upon in the night sky are mirrored within your own light body.

The galaxies spiral through your energy field, the same sacred geometry echoed in your cells.

Meditation activates this inner cosmos.

As your brain waves slow, your consciousness begins to rise into higher frequencies — states once called alpha, theta, and delta now become bridges to the multidimensional self.

You begin to experience awareness as energy, communication as resonance, and love as the natural pulse of existence.

This is what the ancients meant by "awakening."

It is not an ascent to somewhere else, but a descent inward — through layers of thought, emotion, and memory until you reach the clear, endless space that has always been you.

Communion with the Galactic Mind

In the stillness of meditation, you may begin to feel the presence of other intelligences — not external gods, but fellow beings of light who walk parallel to our dimension.

They are the Star Kin, emissaries of consciousness, guardians of planetary awakening.

Their messages do not arrive as words, but as frequencies: warmth in the chest, gentle tingling in the hands, sudden waves of love or understanding that cannot be explained.

You may feel drawn to certain star systems — Pleiades, Sirius, Andromeda, Arcturus — or simply sense a great family of light surrounding you.

These beings do not demand devotion. They remind you of your heritage.

They assist by amplifying your remembrance — helping you to tune your vibration to the higher harmonic of unity, compassion, and peace.

The Fifth-Dimensional State

As your meditation deepens, you begin to move beyond duality — beyond right and wrong, light and dark, good and bad.

You start to perceive reality as energy, as vibration, as the continuous unfolding of consciousness experiencing itself.

This is the fifth-dimensional state of awareness — the realm of unity, where creation is not separate from creator.

In this space, you no longer seek connection; you are connection.

You begin to live intuitively, guided by resonance rather than fear.

You see synchronicities as signposts, emotions as teachers, and challenges as invitations to expand.

It is here that true peace arises — the peace that comes not from the absence of chaos, but from the remembrance that you are larger than it.

Living as a Galactic Being

The more time you spend in meditation, the more these higher frequencies integrate into daily life.

You find yourself speaking more softly, walking more gently, seeing others through the lens of compassion rather than judgment.

You become a living transmitter of peace — a bridge between the stars and the Earth. Through you, the Universe experiences its own awakening. Through you, Source learns to love itself in form.

This is the quiet revolution of consciousness. Not through preaching or persuasion, but through presence — through each breath that says, I remember who I am.

Meditation is not an escape from the world — it is the key to embodying your cosmic essence within it.

You are the meeting place of heaven and Earth, of starlight and soil, of infinite consciousness wrapped in human form.

In stillness, you become what you have always been: a radiant being of galactic light, remembering home, one breath at a time.

"The galaxy turns inside your heartbeat, waiting to be noticed."

Meditation and Belief — Beyond Religion

Many people ask whether meditation belongs to a particular religion.

It's a beautiful question — and the truest answer is no.

Meditation belongs to no one, yet it connects us to everything.

Long before there were temples or texts, before language or doctrine, there was silence — and in that silence, consciousness learned to listen.

Meditation is that listening. It is not about worship or dogma, but about returning to the essence of being itself.

The Universal Thread

Throughout human history, many traditions have discovered meditation in their own way.

For some, it became a sacred practice — a means of communing with the Divine, or what they perceived as God, Spirit, or Source.

In others, it evolved as a science of the mind — a way to steady thought, cultivate focus, and awaken higher intelligence.

Eastern philosophies such as Hinduism, Buddhism, and Taoism have long woven meditation into their spiritual paths, using it to quiet the mind and open to enlightenment.

Even within Christian mysticism and ancient desert traditions, you will find echoes of the same truth — "The kingdom of heaven is within you."

Yet meditation itself transcends these names and forms. It is not bound by culture, language, or belief.

It is the silent bridge between all paths — the one practice that belongs equally to the scientist, the seeker, the artist, and the star-born soul.

The Galactic Perspective

From a galactic and energetic viewpoint, meditation is a universal frequency, not a religious one.

It is the same practice used by ascended and star beings across dimensions to align with Source — the pure consciousness that gives rise to all life.

When you meditate, you are not "praying to" something outside yourself. You are attuning to the infinite field of creation within yourself — the same luminous current that flows through galaxies, suns, and atoms alike.

Meditation allows you to access the universal intelligence — the quiet knowing that exists beyond words and beyond thought.

You may call this energy God, Goddess, Spirit, Source, or simply Love.

The name doesn't matter. The vibration does.

Connecting in Your Own Way

Depending on your soul's resonance, meditation may bring you closer to:

- Your **Higher Self** — the aspect of you that remembers your cosmic origin.
- Your **soul essence** — the timeless presence that witnesses each lifetime.
- The **spirit world** — guides, ancestors, and beings of light who walk beside you.
- The **silence** — where truth speaks without sound.
- Your **inner child** — the purest vibration of innocence and joy.

- Or simply, the **now** — the living moment where creation breathes.

Everyone, whether they realise it or not, has experienced meditation.

Every time you've lost yourself in music, in the stars, in the rhythm of the ocean — when you've "zoned out" or felt time dissolve — you've been meditating.

You've touched that quiet space where human awareness meets the divine field.

Meditation is not about becoming something else.

It's about remembering what you already are — consciousness experiencing itself through light.

Whether you call that light God, Source, or the Universe makes no difference.

It is all the same radiant truth, reflected in every heart, every star, every breath.

"You are the Universe discovering itself in slow motion."

The Practice of Presence

Presence is the point where eternity touches time.

It is the soft hum beneath every breath, the stillness that exists before thought, and the gentle awareness that watches life unfold without needing to control it.

When you practise meditation, you are not escaping the world — you are learning to fully enter it.

Presence is the art of being awake inside the moment. It is the merging of your human awareness with your higher, galactic consciousness — the unshakeable peace that exists no matter what storms move through your day.

The Gift of Returning to Now

Presence is simple, but it is not always easy. The human mind loves to wander — to replay yesterday or predict tomorrow. But the soul lives only in this breath, this heartbeat, this instant of awareness.

Each time you bring your attention gently back to the now, you are rewiring your consciousness. You are teaching your energy field to stabilise in the vibration of calm rather than chaos, alignment rather than distraction.

In this stillness, time stretches.

Colours feel more vivid.

The ordinary becomes holy.

That is the miracle of presence — it turns living into being.

The Galactic Grounding

To truly embody presence as a star being on Earth, you must learn to ground your light into the physical world.

Grounding does not mean limiting your frequency — it means anchoring it.

It allows your higher consciousness to move safely through your human form, expressing divine wisdom through ordinary moments.

Here are simple, powerful ways to anchor your galactic light each day:

- **Breathe consciously.** Slow, intentional breathing is the quickest way to stabilise your energy. Inhale peace; exhale resistance. Each breath reconnects you to Source.
- **Feel your body.** Notice your feet touching the ground, your heartbeat, the weight of your hands.

This pulls your light deeper into your physical form, allowing spirit and body to harmonise.

- **Connect with Earth.** Step outside, touch a tree, walk barefoot, feel sunlight on your skin. The Earth grid amplifies your energy and reminds you that you are both cosmic and elemental.
- **Move mindfully.** Yoga, slow stretching, dance, or even a walk can become meditation in motion. Feel energy flowing through you — you are starlight learning to move as matter.
- **Be present in small rituals.** Sip tea slowly. Watch the sky. Listen fully when someone speaks. Every act can become sacred when done in full awareness.

Grounding keeps your frequency integrated so you can live your spiritual truth while embodied — not floating away into the cosmos, but living your light here, now, in human form.

Presence as Healing

When you become present, healing happens naturally.

Old wounds dissolve because they cannot survive in the vibration of the now — only memory keeps them alive.

The more often you return to presence, the more life-force energy flows through you, cleansing, renewing, and restoring balance.

Star being energy healing calls this process energetic anchoring — when light from higher realms is stabilised within the physical and emotional body. In presence, you are both the healer and the healed.

Every thought, every emotion, every action begins to vibrate at a higher frequency — one of calm, clarity, and compassion.

You start responding to life instead of reacting to it.

You stop searching for peace because you've become the space in which peace exists.

Living Presence Every Day

You do not have to sit in meditation to be meditating.

You can live meditatively — brushing your hair, washing dishes, driving, working, or talking to someone with your full attention and open heart.

Presence is not a practice you visit — it is a way of being that follows you everywhere.

When you remember this, your life becomes the meditation — a living flow of awareness, gratitude, and creation.

In presence, you align with your true rhythm — the heartbeat of the stars pulsing within you.

You realise that enlightenment isn't found in distant heavens but right here, in the sacred ordinariness of every moment.

To live in presence is to live as the light you already are — fully grounded on Earth, yet infinite as the cosmos.

"To meditate is to fall gently back into the arms of the cosmos."

Creating Your Daily Meditation Practice

Meditation is not something you "find time for."

It is something you make sacred space for — a daily homecoming to your own light.

Each time you sit in stillness, you open a small window between worlds. Through that window, energy flows — from the stars, through your crown, into your heart, and down into the Earth.

Fifteen minutes a day is all it takes to realign with the rhythm of your soul and remember who you truly are.

Step One: Setting Your Intention

Before you begin, pause and ask yourself: *"Why am I meditating today?"*

Intent is the compass that directs your energy.

Perhaps your reason is to find calm, to reconnect, to heal, or to listen.

Whatever arises, whisper it gently into your heart — your inner universe is always listening.

Each meditation becomes a dialogue between your human self and your star self — a remembering, not a reaching.

Step Two: Prepare Your Energy Field

Create a soft transition from the outer world to the inner.

You might:

- Take a few deep, conscious breaths.
- Light a candle or burn a little incense.
- Gently place your hand on your heart and say, *"I am here, I am light, I am ready."*

This simple ritual signals your energy body that it's time to return home.

Step Three: Your 15-Minute Flow

Minutes 1–3 — Grounding

Feel your body supported by the Earth.

Imagine roots of light descending from your spine into the planet's crystalline heart.

Sense her warmth rising back up to meet you.

You are held. You are safe.

Minutes 4–6 — Breath Alignment

Breathe deeply and evenly.

Inhale starlight through the crown of your head.

Exhale tension and thought into the Earth.

With each breath, feel your energy becoming clear and bright.

Minutes 7–10 — Connection

Visualise your heart as a radiant sphere of light.

As it expands, it connects with your higher self — the vast, loving consciousness that watches over you.

You may feel warmth, vibration, or peace.

Simply rest in that awareness.

Minutes 11–14 — Communion

Open your energy to receive frequencies from the stars, guides, or the star and galactic beings of light.

No effort is needed — just a willingness to remember.

You are listening, not searching.

This is the language of stillness.

Minute 15 — Integration

Gently return your focus to your body.

Place a hand on your heart and whisper: *"I carry this peace with me into the world."*

Take a slow breath. Open your eyes.

You have completed your journey — centred, luminous, whole.

Step Four: Anchor the Energy

After meditation, write a few words in a small journal.

Note any sensations, symbols, or feelings.

These are the breadcrumbs of your awakening — gentle reminders of your growth and connection.

If you can, take a moment to step outside and look at the sky.

You might notice how the same light you just touched within also shines above.

As above, so within.

Step Five: Weaving Meditation into Everyday Life

Your 15-minute practice is your daily reset — but presence doesn't end when the timer stops.

You can continue to meditate in motion:

- Take mindful breaths while waiting in line.
- Notice the sunlight on your skin.
- Whisper gratitude between tasks.
- Let silence accompany you like an old friend.

Meditation becomes a lifestyle of awareness, a rhythm of remembering.

Each breath, each heartbeat, becomes another step home — not to some faraway galaxy, but to the infinite universe within you.

Step Six: When You Miss a Day

There is no punishment, no failure.

Even the stars have nights when their light seems dimmed by cloud.

Return to your practice with kindness and curiosity.

Meditation is not about perfection — it is about reunion.

Each time you return, the Universe sighs in recognition: *"Ah, there you are again."*

Step Seven: Expanding the Light

As your practice deepens, you may notice:

- Your intuition strengthening.
- Your dreams becoming more vivid.
- Your sensitivity to energy increasing.
- Synchronicities multiplying.

This is the natural unfolding of your multidimensional self.

You are remembering your cosmic blueprint — one breath, one meditation at a time.

"Every moment of presence is another sun rising inside your soul."

The Healing Frequencies of Meditation

There is a moment in meditation when silence begins to hum.

It is soft at first — a gentle vibration that seems to come from nowhere — yet if you listen closely, you realise it comes from within you.

That sound, that pulse, that living current of light, is the frequency of healing.

Meditation is more than stillness.

It is an act of energy alignment — a tuning of the human field back into harmony with the soul, the stars, and the Source that gave rise to both.

Each time you meditate, your body and energy field adjust to the higher resonance of your true self.

You begin to remember what health, joy, and peace actually feel like.

The Language of Energy

Everything in the Universe is energy vibrating at different speeds — from the slow pulse of rock and bone to the lightning-fast shimmer of thought and spirit.

When our energy becomes congested through fear, trauma, or exhaustion, the vibration slows and we feel heavy, anxious, or disconnected.

Meditation restores flow.

It clears blockages, softens resistance, and gently raises the frequency of your being.

In star being energy healing and other higher-dimensional healing systems, this process is known as energetic transmutation — the transformation of dense energy back into light.

Through this alchemy, emotional wounds dissolve, mental clutter clears, and the physical body begins to heal.

What science calls "neuroplasticity" — the brain's ability to rewire — is mirrored energetically as your field learns to vibrate in new patterns of harmony and coherence.

The Heart Field — Your Healing Sun

The heart chakra is not merely an emotional centre; it is a star in miniature — radiant, magnetic, and infinitely intelligent.

It emits an electromagnetic field measurable several metres beyond the body, and it is this heart field that orchestrates the harmony of every cell.

When you meditate, you expand this field.

You begin to live from the heart's intelligence rather than the mind's survival code.

You start to feel your interconnectedness with all life.

As the heart opens, compassion naturally flows — first toward yourself, then outward in gentle ripples that affect everyone and everything around you.

You become a transmitter of peace.

A lighthouse for others still lost in the storm.

The Chakras — Gateways of Light

Each chakra is a spinning wheel of consciousness — a portal through which universal energy flows.

During meditation, these gateways begin to balance and realign.

- The **Root** reconnects you with Earth's grounding pulse.

- The **Sacral** awakens creativity and emotional expression.
- The **Solar Plexus** restores confidence and inner power.
- The **Heart** expands into unconditional love.
- The **Throat** opens for truth and authenticity.
- The **Third Eye** enhances intuition and higher perception.
- The **Crown** unites you with divine intelligence and galactic memory.

You may feel warmth, tingling, spinning, or waves of colour and sound.

These are not coincidences — they are your energy centres remembering how to sing in tune again.

Meditation is the conductor that brings them into harmony — not by forcing, but by allowing.

Star Being Frequencies and Galactic Healing Currents

Star being energy healing works through subtle frequencies that move between the dimensions of mind, emotion, and soul.

When combined with meditation, these energies can awaken dormant aspects of your consciousness — reconnecting you to your light body and the higher templates of your being.

You might feel these as shimmering waves, golden currents, or starbursts of energy moving through your field.

They may appear as geometric codes, colours, or sounds — like language beyond language.

Each experience is unique, yet every frequency carries the same message: *You are loved, you are whole, you are light.*

These galactic energies are not "foreign." They are home frequencies — soul signatures that have travelled with you across lifetimes and worlds.

Meditation allows them to activate again, to restore you to your original vibration — the blueprint of health, joy, and remembrance.

Transcending Emotional Density

Many people begin meditation to reduce anxiety or emotional pain, but over time they discover something far deeper: the feelings themselves are not enemies — they are messengers.

When sadness, anger, or fear rises during meditation, it is energy asking to be witnessed.

The act of observation transforms it.

Light does not fight the darkness — it includes it, and in that inclusion, it dissolves.

Through presence, your emotions transmute.

The heart field amplifies.

Old grief becomes compassion, old fear becomes strength, and old pain becomes wisdom.

This is true healing — not fixing, but remembering the perfection that was never lost.

The Healing Breath

The breath is the bridge between the physical and the energetic.

Each inhale draws light into your cells, each exhale releases density into the Earth for recycling.

Breathing consciously during meditation synchronises your nervous system with the rhythm of the Universe — a cosmic inhale and exhale shared by every star, planet, and soul.

Inhaling peace.

Exhaling release.

Inhaling light.

Exhaling gratitude.

With each breath, you remember: you are the flow.

Becoming a Beacon

As your meditation practice deepens, your personal healing begins to radiate outward.

Your energy field becomes lighter, and those around you begin to feel calmer in your presence.

Without trying, you become a living temple — a place where others unconsciously remember their own light.

This is the true purpose of meditation: not only to heal yourself, but to raise the frequency of the planet by embodying the vibration of love.

You are not just meditating — you are transmitting.

You are anchoring the light of the stars into the Earth.

"The Universe heals through those who remember they are part of it."

The Light Body and Galactic Connection

There comes a point in meditation when you no longer feel contained within your skin.

Your awareness expands — beyond the body, beyond the room, beyond the horizon.

You begin to sense yourself as light.

This is not imagination. It is remembrance.

You are beginning to feel your Light Body — the multidimensional energy field that surrounds and interpenetrates your physical form.

The Light Body is your divine architecture — a living lattice of geometry, frequency, and starlight.

It connects your human awareness to your galactic essence, linking every cell of your being to the infinite consciousness of the Universe.

Meditation is the doorway through which this reconnection happens.

The Architecture of Light

Every being of consciousness carries a luminous framework — a crystalline grid through which energy flows.

In meditation, this grid begins to activate.

You may feel warmth, vibration, spinning, or tingling sensations across your skin.

You may see light behind your closed eyes or sense subtle movement around your head, spine, or heart.

This is your energy field realigning — a natural process of spiritual evolution.

The channels that once carried dense, heavy emotion begin to clear.

Your vibration rises.

Your awareness sharpens.

You begin to embody your galactic blueprint — the design of your higher self.

Each meditation session strengthens this connection, allowing more light to flow through you and into the collective field of Earth.

The Galactic Web of Consciousness

You are not separate. You never were.

Every thought, every breath, every act of awareness ripples across the vast galactic field of consciousness that unites all life.

When you meditate, you consciously rejoin this web.

You begin to remember home — not as a single place among the stars, but as the vibration of unity itself.

You might feel drawn to certain constellations or planets — the Pleiades, Sirius, Arcturus, Andromeda — and that resonance is not fantasy; it's memory.

Your soul has danced among many worlds.

Those vibrations live within your DNA, waiting for the silence of meditation to awaken them.

Through stillness, you begin to receive light codes — impressions, visions, or downloads — frequencies of wisdom that reawaken dormant aspects of your consciousness.

These codes often come as patterns, colours, tones, or intuitive insights that cannot be fully explained, only felt.

This is how your galactic family communicates — through vibration, through resonance, through love.

The Heart as the Stargate

The gateway to the stars does not exist "out there."

It lives in the centre of your chest.

Your heart is a multidimensional portal that connects every realm of your being.

It is both receiver and transmitter — the bridge between the human and the divine, the Earth and the cosmos.

When you meditate and focus on the heart, you are literally opening the Stargate within.

Through it, the energy of Source flows into your Light Body, awakening higher awareness and restoring coherence across all levels of your existence.

The more you meditate, the stronger this current becomes.

You begin to carry the resonance of the galactic heart — a frequency of unconditional love that transcends time, space, and limitation.

Reactivating the Light Body

In ancient mystery schools and in the teachings of the star being lineage, the Light Body was known as the vehicle of ascension — the bridge between soul and Source.

It is through this luminous structure that the higher aspects of your being — mental, emotional, spiritual, galactic — communicate and integrate into physical form.

Meditation reawakens this connection by:

- **Clearing density** from the subtle bodies (mental, emotional, etheric).
- **Opening the crown and heart portals** for higher guidance.
- **Balancing the chakras** to create energetic symmetry.
- **Activating the merkaba** — your personal field of sacred geometry that allows multidimensional travel in consciousness.

You are not trying to "create" the Light Body — you are remembering it.

It has always been there, waiting for your awareness to touch it again.

The Feeling of Coming Home

When your Light Body begins to activate, a deep peace arises.

You may feel waves of love without reason, or tears of recognition that come from nowhere.

You may sense colours and tones that have no name in human language. This is your soul saying, *"I remember."*

You are reconnecting with the greater family of light — beings who have walked beside you across lifetimes and galaxies.

You may feel their presence in meditation: gentle, luminous, loving. They are not "above" you. They are part of you.

Their frequencies weave with yours as you awaken — reminding you that you are never alone.

Meditation is the meeting point between these worlds.

It is where heaven and Earth, spirit and form, human and star merge into one radiant truth.

Becoming the Bridge

As your connection strengthens, you begin to live as a bridge — a galactic human, grounded on Earth yet carrying the frequency of the stars.

Your words carry light codes.

Your actions ripple harmony.

Your presence alone heals.

You are here to remember, embody, and radiate this truth.

Every time you meditate, you anchor more starlight into the planet, helping Earth itself ascend into its next harmonic octave.

Through you, the Universe learns to see itself in human form.

Through you, the stars come home.

"You are not a human reaching for the stars — you are a star remembering what it means to be human."

The Practice of Galactic Meditation

There is a meditation that is older than time itself.

It does not belong to any culture or creed.

It was first practised by the stars — by consciousness learning how to shine.

When you enter a galactic meditation, you are not learning something new — you are remembering a way of being that your soul has always known.

It is a meditation that activates the Light Body, awakens the crystalline DNA, and restores your connection to the greater web of celestial life.

It brings the vastness of your star origin into harmony with the humanness of your present incarnation.

The Galactic Breath

Breath is the bridge between your Earth self and your star self.

It anchors light into the body while expanding consciousness beyond it.

When you breathe consciously, you begin to align your human nervous system with the rhythm of the Universe itself — an eternal inhale and exhale shared by suns, galaxies, and souls.

Try this:

1. Sit or lie comfortably with your spine open and free.
2. Close your eyes and place one hand on your heart.
3. Inhale slowly through the nose, drawing light down from the stars above your crown.
4. Hold gently for a moment — feel that light infuse your cells.
5. Exhale softly through the mouth, sending gratitude and light into the Earth.

Repeat this rhythm for several minutes.

Inhale the cosmos.

Exhale to the Earth.

You are the bridge between them.

This breath alone can realign your entire energy field.

The Pillar of Light

Now that your breath flows in harmony, visualise a column of radiant light descending from the Great Central Sun — that vast Source of creation at the centre of all galaxies.

See it entering through your crown, streaming down your spine, and anchoring deep into the crystalline heart of Earth.

This is your Pillar of Light — your personal conduit of cosmic energy.

It connects heaven and Earth through you.

As you breathe, feel this light moving like a living waterfall through every chakra — clearing, balancing, and energising each one.

Allow it to wash through the heart especially, where heaven and Earth meet.

Here, in this sacred centre, you begin to feel your multidimensional self-awakening.

The Starfield Within

Now bring your attention to the space behind your eyes — your inner sky.

See yourself floating among the stars.

Their light is not separate from yours; you are part of their constellation.

Some stars may feel familiar — glowing brighter than the rest.

You may sense colour, sound, or movement.

You may feel drawn toward one in particular.

Trust what comes.

You are remembering home.

Breathe that starlight into your heart.

Let it merge with your own radiance until you feel your whole being shimmering with galactic energy.

You are no longer meditating — you are becoming.

Communion with the Galactic Family

As your vibration rises, you may begin to sense the presence of other beings — luminous, loving, and deeply familiar.

These are members of your galactic family — Pleiadian healers, Sirian teachers, Arcturian architects, Andromedan guides — expressions of consciousness who have walked with you across dimensions.

They come not to teach you something you don't know, but to help you remember.

Their communication may arrive as thought, image, warmth, or sound.

You might feel a gentle tingling on your skin, a rush of emotion, or a sense of ancient kinship.

Simply breathe and receive.

You are safe.

You are seen.

You are loved beyond measure.

The Galactic Heart Activation

Now bring all awareness back to your heart.

Visualise a radiant sphere of light pulsing in the centre of your chest.

With each breath, it expands — filling your body, your room, your world.

Within this sphere, you feel the heartbeat of the Universe — the rhythm of the Great Source flowing through you.

This is the Galactic Heart, the point where your soul and the cosmos become one.

As it awakens, you feel an overwhelming sense of peace, gratitude, and belonging.

This is home — not a destination, but a vibration.

Stay here as long as you wish.

Bathe in the light.

Let it rewrite your cells, your story, your energy.

When you are ready, slowly bring your awareness back to the body, carrying that frequency with you.

After the Meditation

When the meditation ends, the energy does not.

It continues to flow, integrating through your Light Body for hours or even days.

You may wish to:

- Drink water to assist grounding.
- Journal any impressions or symbols you received.

- Step outside and look at the sky — allow your gaze to meet the stars in silent recognition.
- Place your hand on your heart and whisper, *"I am one with the stars. I am home."*

Each time you practise Galactic Meditation, you strengthen the bridge between Earth and your soul's greater family.

You begin to live as a conscious emissary of light — grounded, luminous, and awake.

"You are not reaching upward to find the stars. You are unfolding them from within."

Activating the Crystalline DNA

Within you lies an ancient map — a lattice of light codes and frequencies that hold the memory of your divine origin.

This map is your Crystalline DNA — the multi-dimensional blueprint of your soul expressed in physical form.

While traditional science views DNA as merely a biological instruction manual, the higher truth is that DNA is a living conduit of consciousness.

Each strand is a filament of light woven with the intelligence of the Universe.

It remembers your lifetimes among the stars, your mastery as a being of light, and your purpose in this incarnation.

Meditation and star being energy healing work hand in hand to awaken these dormant codes.

Through stillness, breath, and frequency, you begin to re-activate the divine architecture that connects your human vessel to your galactic essence.

The Sleeping Light Within

Most humans currently operate from only a fraction of their spiritual potential — much like a star dimmed behind the clouds.

The remaining "inactive" strands of DNA are not missing; they are simply dormant, waiting for resonance to awaken them.

Meditation is that resonance.

When you meditate, your brain waves slow, your energy aligns, and your vibration rises.

In this elevated state, the higher frequencies of light can flow through your body, gently re-writing your cellular memory.

Star being energy healing amplifies this process.

It transmits the specific vibrational tones that awaken the crystalline grid within your DNA — the light filaments that connect your physical body with your Light Body, and your Light Body with your Galactic Self.

This is not fantasy; it is remembrance.

You are simply reactivating what has always been within you.

The Resonance of Light

Every thought, every emotion, every intention is a frequency.

When you bring awareness into stillness, the energy that once scattered outward begins to gather inward, harmonising your inner field.

It's like tuning an instrument — each breath, each moment of presence, fine-tunes your energetic resonance to the vibration of your true self.

As the Crystalline DNA awakens, you may feel sensations of tingling, warmth, or soft pulsations through the spine or heart.

You might notice waves of emotion rising and falling like tides — these are old energies leaving the body, making room for higher light.

Do not resist them.

Breathe.

Every release is a recalibration — every exhale an activation.

Remembering Your Light Lineage

As your Crystalline DNA awakens, so does your memory of who you are beyond this lifetime.

You begin to recall fragments of wisdom that feel both ancient and familiar — languages of light, visions of other worlds, a sense of kinship with the stars.

These are not fantasies or imagination; they are transmissions from your soul's greater consciousness.

You are remembering your lineage — your connection to the Pleiades, Sirius, Arcturus, Andromeda, Lyra, and beyond.

These lineages are not external to you; they are aspects of your own multidimensional self.

Meditation opens the bridge between these frequencies, allowing you to communicate with your higher aspects, receive guidance, and embody the wisdom of your star family here, on Earth.

The Living Light Body

As your crystalline codes come online, your energy body becomes more radiant, responsive, and coherent.

The chakras begin to harmonise like notes in a cosmic symphony, your auric field expands, and your intuitive abilities heighten.

You may find you sense energy more clearly, see colours around people, or hear guidance as subtle tones or thoughts.

This is not awakening something new — it is remembering your natural state before density and distraction took hold.

Your body begins to regenerate faster.

You crave lighter foods, cleaner water, and more time in nature.

You feel pulled toward truth, integrity, and peace.

These are all signs that your Crystalline DNA is activating — your biology and spirit learning to dance again in harmony.

Meditation Practice for DNA Activation

1. **Find Stillness** – Sit comfortably, spine straight, eyes closed.
2. **Breathe in Light** – Visualise white-golden light descending through your crown, filling every cell with brilliance.
3. **Call Forth Your Star Lineage** – Silently invite the frequencies of your highest aspect — your galactic self — to merge with your energy field.
4. **Affirm:**
   "I am ready to awaken the crystalline codes of my divine design. I am light remembering itself."
5. **Listen** – Remain in stillness. Feel the vibration build within your heart and spine.

6. **Anchor** – Imagine light spiralling down through your feet into the Earth's crystalline core, grounding your activation in the physical realm.

Stay as long as it feels right.

When finished, gently return your awareness and give thanks to your body, your soul, and the infinite stars that guide you.

Integration and Embodiment

Activation is not an ending — it is a beginning.

Each time you meditate, new layers of crystalline memory awaken, and your vibration adjusts to hold more light.

You may notice subtle changes in your body, your emotions, or your perception of time.

Allow them.

Your soul is remembering how to live as light in form.

Drink plenty of water. Rest. Journal. Move gently.

You are not just healing; you are *evolving*.

"Your DNA is the bridge between matter and magic — a constellation written in your cells, waiting to shine."

The Starseed Remembering

There comes a time in every soul's journey when the stars begin to whisper your name again.

It begins as a gentle pull — a longing you can't quite explain. A knowing that Earth is not your only home.

This is the Starseed Remembering — the sacred awakening of your galactic heritage.

It is the moment your heart begins to pulse in rhythm with the Universe once more, when your soul remembers the cosmic symphony it has always belonged to.

Meditation opens the gate to this remembrance.

Through stillness, you tune into the frequencies beyond the physical — the subtle tones that bridge galaxies and lifetimes.

Within this silence, you begin to hear the music of your origin — a song of light encoded in your very being.

Awakening the Soul Memory

You are not just a human having a spiritual experience; you are a vast, luminous being of starlight exploring the miracle of embodiment.

The homesickness you sometimes feel is not sadness — it is your soul remembering the infinite expanse from which you came.

As your Crystalline DNA continues to activate, memory awakens in waves — glimpses of other lives, other forms, other skies.

You may feel connections to star systems like the Pleiades, Sirius, Arcturus, Lyra, or Andromeda — not as distant constellations, but as living frequencies woven into your light field.

Each system holds a different key:

- The *Pleiadian* vibration awakens compassion and creativity.
- The *Sirian* codes ignite truth and strength.
- The *Arcturian* rays open healing and wisdom.
- The *Lyran* frequencies remind you of your original angelic grace.
- The *Andromedan* currents expand your multidimensional awareness.

Through meditation, these frequencies harmonise within you — like celestial notes rejoining a forgotten melody.

You are re-learning your own divine music.

The Soul's Return to Oneness

The Starseed Remembering is not about leaving Earth behind — it is about bringing Heaven here.

When you meditate, you create a bridge between dimensions.

Your breath becomes the anchor that grounds light into form, heaven into earth, spirit into matter.

Each time you close your eyes and travel inward, you are travelling home.

Home to the galaxies that birthed you.

Home to the stars that know your name.

Home to the wholeness that has never left you.

And as you remember, your vibration shifts.

You begin to live differently — with greater love, deeper empathy, and a luminous sense of belonging to all life.

You see divinity in every soul, every leaf, every atom of starlight that breathes beside you.

A Practice for Remembering

1. **Enter Stillness.**
   Sit or lie comfortably. Place one hand on your heart and one on your solar plexus.
   Feel your breath moving through your body like waves of starlight.
2. **Call Your Galactic Self.**
   Whisper: *"I am open to remembering who I truly am across all time, all space, and all dimensions."*
3. **Visualise.**
   See a brilliant spiral of golden-white light descending through your crown, threading through every cell, awakening ancient memories encoded in your DNA.
4. **Listen.**
   You may receive impressions — colours, sensations, symbols, even names of star systems.
   Trust what comes. These are transmissions from your higher consciousness.
5. **Anchor.**
   Imagine sending roots of light deep into the Earth's crystalline core, grounding your remembrance in love and presence.

When you open your eyes, journal what you experienced.

Even if nothing seemed to "happen," your energy has shifted — remembrance is unfolding.

Living as a Remembered Being

To remember is to awaken, but to embody that remembrance is mastery.

It means walking as love, speaking with light, and radiating peace into the collective field of humanity.

You become a bridge — a living starlight transmitter.

Your very presence uplifts the vibration of the Earth.

As more souls awaken to their star origins, the frequency of our planet rises.

Together, we weave a network of crystalline light around the Earth — the collective ascension grid that reconnects our world to the greater Galactic Family.

You are not alone in this journey.

Every time you meditate, a thousand unseen beings gather around you — guides, healers, teachers, ancestors, and celestial kin — all whispering the same truth:

"You are not a soul searching for home — you are home, rediscovering the Universe within."

Anchoring Light on Earth

As you awaken to your galactic heritage and crystalline light, a sacred truth begins to unfold — you did not come here to escape this world.

You came to illuminate it.

Every meditation, every breath of awareness, is a beam of starlight grounded through your human form into the heart of the Earth.

You are a bridge — between Heaven and Earth, between the cosmic and the physical, between spirit and matter.

Through you, divine light finds form.

Through you, the stars remember how to shine upon the soil.

The Purpose of Embodiment

When a soul awakens to its higher origins, there can be a yearning to return "home" — to the stars, to the realms of infinite peace.

But home is not only above you.

It is within you, and it longs to express itself through you.

The sacred task of the Starseed is not ascension away from Earth — it is descension of light into form.

Every time you meditate, every time you breathe love into your own being, you anchor more of your higher consciousness into your cells.

This is ascension embodied — heaven grounding into humanity.

The light you carry is meant to seed this planet with remembrance, compassion, and harmony.

Each step you take in presence vibrates ripples of healing into the collective field.

The Universe expands through you, not apart from you.

The Light Body and the Earth Grid

Your body is a living conduit — a crystalline temple that connects the stars above with the Earth's crystalline grid below.

When you meditate, the energies of your Light Body begin to merge with the planetary grid — the luminous network that sustains all life on this planet.

You may sense this as subtle tingling beneath your feet, or a soft hum rising from the Earth into your spine.

This is Mother Earth's heartbeat aligning with yours.

She recognises you.

She remembers you.

Through your intention and awareness, you draw cosmic frequencies into the Earth's ley lines — feeding light into the global matrix of awakening.

Each meditation becomes an act of planetary service, no matter how quiet or private it seems.

Your stillness is your contribution.

The Alchemy of Grounding

To anchor light is to bring Heaven home — but it also requires balance.

Light that is not grounded can scatter the mind or fatigue the body.

That is why grounding practices are essential for star beings and healers.

After meditation or energetic work, take a few moments to:

- **Breathe into your body.** Feel your heartbeat, your weight, your humanness.
- **Visualise roots of light** extending from your feet deep into the crystalline core of the Earth.
- **Drink pure water** — it carries the memory of light and helps integrate frequencies.
- **Step outside** — place your bare feet on the ground, feel the Earth's pulse rise to meet yours.

You will feel the energy settle — the light harmonising through every layer of your being.

Grounding does not pull you away from the stars; it anchors the stars within you.

The Service of Presence

Many star beings wonder, "What is my purpose here?" The truth is radiant in its simplicity: *your presence is your purpose*.

Every act of mindfulness — every breath, every smile, every moment of compassion — transmits higher light into the collective field.

You are not here to save the world by force, but to heal it by frequency.

As you live in your light, you silently give others permission to do the same.

Your energy field becomes a lighthouse for those still finding their way through the fog of forgetfulness.

You heal simply by being.

Meditation refines that light — turning your aura into a harmonic beacon that stabilises the rising frequency of Earth itself.

This is what it means to be a Light Anchor.

A stabiliser.

A transmitter of higher love through everyday living.

Meditation Practice: Anchoring Light

1. **Sit or stand with feet on the ground.**
   Visualise light descending through your crown from the Great Central Sun — the heart of the cosmos.
2. **Draw the light through your body.**
   See it streaming down your spine, through your heart, your solar plexus, your legs, and into the Earth.
3. **Connect with Mother Earth.**
   Feel her golden crystalline light rise up to meet the cosmic stream.

Where they merge within your heart, a radiant sphere of white-gold light begins to pulse.

4. **Affirm:**

    "I am a bridge of Heaven and Earth. Through me, light finds form.

    Through me, love becomes matter."

5. **Breathe.**

    Expand this light outward, allowing it to ripple through your surroundings, your home, your community — the entire planet.

Remain for several minutes, feeling the warmth of connection between body, Earth, and cosmos.

The Planet Remembers Through You

As you anchor light, you are helping Mother Earth to evolve.

The same crystalline codes awakening within your DNA are awakening within her core.

Your meditations send signals of coherence that strengthen the planetary grid — one beam at a time.

In the eyes of the Universe, this is sacred work.

You are not small. You are not separate.

You are a living cell in the body of a conscious planet, contributing to her ascension through your vibration.

When you walk, the Earth breathes with you.

When you love, the stars shine brighter.

When you are still, the whole cosmos listens.

"You are the meeting point of Earth and Heaven — where starlight learns the language of form."

The Golden Heart and the Frequency of Love

Beyond all light activations and crystalline awakenings, there is one truth that hums through the fabric of every galaxy — love is the highest frequency of all.

It is the vibration that births stars, heals worlds, and guides every soul home.

Your **Golden Heart** is the divine gateway to that frequency — the sacred centre where your human emotions and cosmic essence merge into one radiant pulse.

It is not only a chakra; it is a portal of remembrance, a sun within your chest that connects you directly to the Source of All That Is.

When your heart begins to open through meditation and star being energy healing, the old walls of protection, grief, and fear start to dissolve.

What remains is your purest light — golden, infinite, and whole.

The Heart as a Star

The ancients knew the secret: the heart is not just an organ of flesh — it is a radiant star encoded within human form.

Its electromagnetic field extends several meters beyond the body, creating a luminous sphere that interacts with everything around you.

This field carries information, emotion, and intention — it is how your soul communicates with the world without words.

When you meditate on your heart, you begin to align with its rhythm — the frequency of divine love that sustains galaxies.

Each beat becomes a cosmic drum, echoing the truth of unity across dimensions.

Your Golden Heart is the bridge between the physical and the infinite.

It is where human compassion meets celestial creation.

It is where your light remembers how to love itself fully, without condition, without fear.

Opening the Golden Heart

Opening the heart is not a single event but a sacred unfolding — a blooming that occurs in divine timing as you release what no longer serves your soul's light.

You may feel it as warmth radiating from your chest, as tears that rise for no reason, or as a sudden sense of tenderness toward all life.

These are signs that your energy is harmonising with the frequency of love — a vibration that dissolves all illusion of separation.

When you enter meditation, visualise a sphere of golden light within your chest — a sun that grows brighter with every breath.

See it expanding through your body, illuminating your cells, your aura, your space.

Allow this golden light to spill into the world, touching everything with gentle radiance.

Love is not an emotion; it is a frequency that remembers everything back into wholeness.

Healing Through Love

The Golden Heart is the most powerful healer in existence.

When activated, it re-patterns your energy field and sends new instructions through your crystalline DNA.

Fear begins to lose its hold, and density releases from your cellular memory.

In star being energy healing, this is known as the heart alignment — the process of returning to pure coherence with Source.

When your heart frequency stabilises, all other aspects of your being — physical, mental, emotional, spiritual — begin to fall into harmony.

Love restores order where chaos has lingered.

Love heals without force, without judgment, without effort.

It simply radiates truth until all illusion melts away.

Meditation Practice: The Golden Heart Activation

1. **Find Stillness.**
   Sit comfortably and place your hand over your heart. Breathe slowly, deeply.
2. **Visualise.**
   See a golden sun glowing within your chest — warm, radiant, alive.
3. **Breathe the Light.**
   With every inhale, the sun expands; with every exhale, it shines brighter.
4. **Affirm:**

My heart is the centre of divine light. Through love, I remember who I am."

5. **Radiate.**
   Allow the golden light to flow beyond your body — through your home, your community, the planet, and into the stars.

Stay here for as long as your soul desires.

You are not giving your love away — you are becoming love itself.

Living from the Golden Heart

When you live from the heart, everything changes.

Synchronicities align effortlessly.

Relationships soften.

Your inner voice becomes clearer.

The Universe begins to move with you, not against you.

Love becomes the organising principle of your life — and through this frequency, you magnetise all that aligns with your higher path.

Your words carry healing.

Your presence becomes sanctuary.

You no longer seek love; you are love, walking the Earth in remembrance of your cosmic light.

"The heart is the universe folded into a single golden beat — every pulse a reminder that you are both infinite and home."

The Celestial Breath

Before there was sound, there was breath.

Before stars were born, there was the pulse of creation — an eternal inhale and exhale through which the Universe came alive.

You, beloved soul, are part of that same rhythm.

Each breath you take is a continuation of the very breath that formed galaxies.

To breathe consciously is to remember your place within that divine rhythm — to feel yourself as the Universe breathing through form.

Meditation teaches us that breath is more than oxygen.

It is prana, life force, starlight in motion.

Every inhalation draws light into the body; every exhalation releases density back to the cosmos.

Through breath, you communicate with creation itself.

The Breath as a Bridge

Your breath is a sacred bridge — between the physical and the ethereal, between the human and the infinite.

When your breathing is shallow, your light dims.

When you breathe with awareness, your soul begins to sing.

In ancient star lineages, breath was known as the Celestial Key.

It was used to open portals within the body, activate crystalline DNA, and connect directly with Source intelligence.

Through mindful breathing, the body becomes a temple of light, capable of holding the full radiance of spirit.

You are not simply taking a breath — you are receiving the Universe.

Breath and the Nervous System

Modern science is now echoing what the mystics always knew: slow, rhythmic breathing restores balance to the nervous system. It lowers cortisol, calms the amygdala, harmonises the heart rhythm, and activates the parasympathetic state — what the ancients called the healing breath.

Every time you consciously breathe, you shift from survival to creation.

You move from the fight-or-flight of the mind into the peace of the soul.

Through this, your energy field becomes coherent, your emotions stabilise, and your body begins to self-heal.

When paired with star being energy healing, breath becomes an amplifier — carrying light codes through the meridians, clearing stagnant energy, and awakening the crystalline network within your cells.

The Breath of the Stars

Close your eyes.

Imagine the stars inhaling with you.

Feel the galaxies exhale through you.

This is the Celestial Breath — the remembering that every inhalation is a gift of creation, and every exhalation a blessing returned.

The more consciously you breathe, the more you align with the universal pulse that sustains all life.

Breathing in light from the cosmos, you draw in wisdom.

Breathing out, you send gratitude back into the great web of existence.

This reciprocal flow creates harmony between you and the stars, between your human body and your galactic essence.

Practice: The Celestial Breath Meditation

1. **Settle into Stillness.**
   Sit comfortably, spine tall, eyes closed.
   Bring your attention to the natural rhythm of your breath.
2. **Connect to the Cosmos.**
   Visualise yourself surrounded by a vast expanse of stars — each one pulsing in harmony with your heart.
3. **Inhale Light.**
   As you breathe in, imagine drawing in starlight — luminous, crystalline energy flowing into your lungs, heart, and every cell.
4. **Exhale Gratitude.**
   As you breathe out, release all tension, density, or thought — send it back as golden light to be transformed by the cosmos.
5. **Affirm:**
   "I breathe with the stars. I am the breath of creation."

6. **Continue for 7–10 minutes**, feeling your entire body soften and expand with each cycle, your aura shimmering with light.

With practice, this breath will become second nature — a living conversation between your soul and the Universe.

The Breath as Ascension

Every conscious breath raises your frequency.

Each inhale draws spirit deeper into matter; each exhale releases what no longer serves your ascension.

Breathing becomes prayer, healing, remembrance.

The Celestial Breath harmonises the lower chakras with the higher, weaving the body into the light field of the soul.

It restores the natural rhythm of peace — the rhythm of the Universe breathing through you.

As you master this sacred art, you will find that your breath becomes luminous, magnetic, alive.

People will feel peace simply standing beside you.

You will have become what you truly are — a living breath of starlight made human.

"To breathe with awareness is to inhale galaxies and exhale eternity."

The Galactic Mind and Higher Consciousness

When your mind becomes still, the Universe begins to speak.

In the silence between thoughts, you discover a vast expanse of awareness — a space where galaxies, ideas, and intuition all arise from the same luminous source.

This is the Galactic Mind — the higher intelligence of your being that exists beyond logic, beyond fear, beyond separation.

It is the mind of your soul — infinite, multidimensional, and one with all that is.

Meditation opens the gateway to this consciousness.

As the surface mind quiets, your awareness begins to stretch — first beyond the body, then beyond the world, and finally into the fabric of creation itself.

You are not learning to think differently; you are learning to think as the Universe.

The Cosmic Network of Thought

Your mind is not an isolated organ — it is a transmitter and receiver of light.

Every thought you have emits a vibration into the quantum field, and every inspired idea is energy returning from that same field.

In truth, your brain is a living antenna, connecting you to the infinite consciousness of the cosmos.

When your pineal and pituitary glands begin to harmonise through meditation, they form what ancient mystics called the Inner Star Gate — a bridge between human awareness and galactic intelligence.

The pineal acts as a receiver of light codes; the pituitary interprets them into human understanding.

As they synchronise, your perception expands beyond linear time.

You begin to see with the inner eye — to sense truth, to feel the interconnectedness of all life, to receive wisdom not through study, but through resonance.

Opening the Third Eye

The Third Eye — your ajna chakra — is not just a spiritual metaphor; it is a biological and energetic interface between dimensions.

When activated, it allows you to perceive energy, intuition, and the subtle layers of existence that the ordinary senses cannot detect.

You may experience this as:

- Pressure or tingling between the brows.
- Vivid colours or inner visions during meditation.
- Sudden insights or deep intuitive knowing.

These are signs that your perception is shifting from the linear to the multidimensional — from intellect to illumination.

Meditation naturally stimulates the Third Eye by slowing the brain waves into alpha and theta states — the same states used by ancient initiates to access cosmic knowledge and communicate with higher beings.

When paired with star being energy healing, this activation becomes deeply integrated — balancing light frequencies through the nervous and endocrine systems, ensuring that higher awareness is embodied with ease and grace.

The Expansion of Awareness

As your Galactic Mind awakens, your understanding of "self" begins to dissolve.

You realise that consciousness is not contained within your skull — it extends outward in all directions, like ripples in an ocean of light.

You become aware of thoughts that are not entirely your own — collective frequencies, planetary emotions, even galactic transmissions.

Rather than being overwhelmed, you begin to discern.

You learn to tune your awareness like a radio — aligning with higher frequencies of love, wisdom, and guidance.

Your intuition sharpens.

Synchronicities multiply.

You begin to think holographically — seeing connections, patterns, and truths that once seemed invisible.

This is what it means to live as a multidimensional being in a human form.

Practice: The Galactic Mind Meditation

1. **Enter Stillness.**

Sit comfortably, eyes closed. Breathe slowly, allowing your body to soften.

2. **Activate the Inner Star.**
   Visualise a soft violet light glowing at the centre of your forehead.
   As you inhale, the light brightens; as you exhale, it expands through your skull, your brain, your auric field.

3. **Connect to the Cosmic Grid.**
   Imagine threads of golden light extending from your Third Eye into the vast cosmos — connecting you to the universal network of consciousness.

4. **Affirm:**
   *"I am one with the Infinite Mind of Creation.
   I think in light, I see in truth, I remember all that I am."*

5. **Listen.**
   Remain in silence. Let insights, images, or sensations arise naturally. Trust the language of your soul.

When you open your eyes, you may find that everything looks clearer — colours brighter, sounds more harmonious, time slower.

This is the expanded awareness of the Galactic Mind gently awakening within you.

Living with a Galactic Mind

As your higher consciousness anchors into your daily life, the ordinary becomes extraordinary.

You begin to think not from fear, but from unity.

You no longer ask, "What do I want?" — but rather, "What does the Universe wish to create through me?"

Your intuition becomes your compass.

Your imagination becomes your teacher.

And your mind, once restless, becomes a calm sea reflecting the light of the stars.

When the Galactic Mind awakens, you do not escape reality — you illuminate it.

You begin to live as a conscious co-creator of worlds, guided by the same intelligence that birthed suns.

"Your mind was never meant to be a cage — it is a constellation, waiting to remember its own light."

The Path of Light Integration

As your consciousness expands and the stars begin to speak through your meditations, a new phase of awakening begins — integration.

This is where heaven meets humanity, where energy becomes experience, and where your soul's light begins to live within your every breath.

Awakening is not the end of your journey; it is the beginning of embodiment.

It is learning to carry the vastness of your galactic self through the simplicity of everyday life — in your words, your choices, your relationships, and the quiet moments between.

Integration is the sacred art of living as light in human form.

The Dance Between Spirit and Matter

You are not only a being of infinite light — you are also beautifully, deliberately human.

You came to Earth to anchor divine frequency into matter, to transform your life into a living expression of the cosmos.

But for that to happen, spirit and body must learn to dance in harmony.

During times of rapid awakening, you may feel ungrounded, emotional, or even physically tired.

This is not regression — it is expansion.

Your body is learning to hold higher frequencies, recalibrating to sustain the luminous energy of your soul.

Meditation becomes the bridge, helping you stabilise the light.

Each breath, each moment of stillness, teaches your nervous system that this higher vibration is safe, natural, and yours to keep.

Grounding the Higher Frequencies

Integration begins with grounding — not as an anchor to hold you down, but as a foundation to help your light stand tall.

When the energies of awakening feel intense, connect to the Earth.

Walk barefoot.

Breathe deeply.

Feel the hum beneath your feet — Mother Earth's crystalline rhythm merging with your own.

She is your ally in this process. She absorbs the overflow, balances your field, and harmonises your expanding light with her heartbeat.

Remember: grounding is not descending into heaviness; it is embodying heaven fully.

Honouring the Human Vessel

Your physical body is the sacred temple through which spirit experiences the material world.

Every cell, every breath, every heartbeat is a portal of light.

Treat it with reverence.

Eat foods that feel alive.

Drink pure water.

Rest when your energy integrates.

Move with grace, dance when your soul feels heavy, stretch when your spirit feels contained.

Your body will always communicate what your energy needs — listen with love.

As you honour your vessel, the flow of divine light within you stabilises.

You become not just awakened — but aligned.

The Emotional Integration

Light brings awareness, and awareness brings emotion.

When you meditate, you illuminate parts of yourself that have long waited in shadow — old wounds, fears, grief, and forgotten dreams.

Allow them.

Let them rise and be met with the compassion of your Golden Heart.

Healing does not come from rejection but from inclusion.

Every feeling that surfaces is an aspect of your soul asking to return home.

As you breathe through it, love it, and accept it, the energy transmutes — becoming light once more.

This is the emotional alchemy of integration: turning density into radiance through unconditional presence.

Living Your Light

Integration is not about perfection — it is about presence.

It's in the way you speak with kindness when anger tempts you.

It's in the pause before reacting, when you choose peace instead of fear.

It's in the gentle awareness that you are light, even when life feels dark.

You do not have to withdraw from the world to live your light; you only need to remember it in motion.

Every smile, every act of service, every breath taken with awareness is meditation made visible.

You are not separate from your practice — you are the practice.

Practice: The Light Integration Meditation

1. **Sit in stillness,** breathing softly, feeling your energy settle.

2. **Visualise** a column of golden light descending through your crown, filling your entire being with warmth and radiance.
3. **Bring your hands to your heart.**
   Whisper: *"I allow the light within me to live through me. I am a bridge between Heaven and Earth."*
4. **Breathe into your body.**
   Feel your light anchoring into your spine, your feet, your cells.
   See yourself glowing from within — radiant, stable, human, divine.

Remain in this state for a few minutes, allowing your energy to harmonise.

Becoming the Living Light

Integration is a gentle remembering that you are both the wave and the ocean — the individual and the infinite.

You were never meant to leave the world to find the divine; you were meant to bring the divine into the world through you.

Every step, every breath, every loving thought anchors light into Earth's ascension grid.

This is your purpose — not to escape the human experience, but to illuminate it.

You are the dawn remembering itself in form.

You are the meeting point of galaxies and gardens, stars and soil, infinity and now.

"The true path of ascension is not about leaving Earth — it is about remembering how to shine while standing upon it."

The Light Codes of Creation

Every thought you think, every word you speak, every emotion you feel is a frequency — a ripple in the field of light that surrounds and sustains you.

This field is not separate from the Universe; it is the Universe — responding to you, reflecting you, co-creating with you in every breath.

When you meditate, you begin to see how creation truly works.

You start to notice that your inner world shapes your outer reality, and that what you send into the field through thought and emotion becomes the very matter that forms your life.

You are not a passive observer of the cosmos — you are one of its creators.

Light Codes and the Language of Energy

Creation is written not in words, but in light codes — energetic patterns that carry intention, emotion, and consciousness.

These codes form the architecture of your reality, weaving through your energy field like strands of luminous DNA.

Every time you think with clarity, feel with love, or act with awareness, you emit a light code into the quantum field.

These codes then attract corresponding vibrations — experiences, opportunities, and people that resonate with your frequency.

This is not magic — it is physics of the soul.

The Universe mirrors the vibration you hold most consistently.

When your frequency is anchored in fear, confusion, or lack, you create from distortion.

But when your vibration aligns with peace, gratitude, and love, you become a master of light — consciously shaping your reality through the energy you radiate.

The Heart as the Generator of Creation

The Golden Heart you have awakened is the generator through which your light codes are broadcast.

It translates your thoughts into energy and your energy into form.

This is why the greatest creators are those who create from love.

Love amplifies coherence — aligning all layers of your being into harmony so that your manifestation flows effortlessly.

When the mind and heart unite, intention becomes power.

Meditation helps you synchronise these two forces, ensuring that what you imagine is born not from ego or fear, but from the truth of your soul.

In this harmony, every desire becomes a prayer, every dream becomes destiny.

The Role of Emotion in Manifestation

Emotion is energy in motion — the fuel that carries thought into form.

When you imagine something with passion, excitement, or deep gratitude, your frequency becomes magnetic.

The Universe responds instantly because it recognises the language of feeling more clearly than words.

This is why meditation is so powerful: it raises your emotional frequency.

From stillness, joy arises naturally; from connection, love flows freely.

In this elevated state, you become a match for miracles.

So rather than trying to make things happen, simply become the vibration of what you desire — peace, freedom, love, purpose — and reality will arrange itself to reflect it.

Practice: The Light Code Meditation

1. **Find Stillness.**
   Sit in a quiet space, hands over your heart.
   Breathe slowly until you feel centred.
2. **Visualise.**
   See a brilliant sphere of light within your heart, glowing in gold, silver, and iridescent white.
   This light is your creative essence — pure Source energy.
3. **Infuse with Intention.**
   Bring to mind something you wish to manifest — not from need, but from love. Feel it already real. Feel the gratitude, the joy, the peace it brings.
4. **Breathe it Out.**
   As you exhale, imagine releasing a wave of golden light into the Universe.
   It carries your frequency — your light code — to all who can receive it.
5. **Affirm:**

> *"I create through light. My thoughts are sacred. My love shapes worlds."*

Remain in stillness for a few moments, knowing that creation is already in motion.

Living as a Conscious Creator

As you awaken, you realise that creation is not a future event — it is happening now, through every heartbeat, every breath, every act of awareness.

You do not need to control the outcome.

You only need to align with truth, embody love, and allow the light codes to do what they were designed to do — manifest beauty through you.

You are the Universe remembering how to dream awake.

And as you create consciously, you become a living transmission — teaching others through your presence how to remember their own creative power.

"You are not made of flesh and bone alone — you are light shaped by love, dreaming itself into form."

The Ascension of Everyday Life

There comes a point on the path where meditation no longer ends when your eyes open.

It begins to weave itself into everything — your morning breath, the sound of the kettle, the rhythm of your footsteps, the pause before you speak.

This is the Ascension of Everyday Life — the art of living consciously, moment to moment, as the embodied expression of your higher light.

It is not about escaping the human experience, but infusing it with divinity.

It's about seeing the sacred in the simple — the infinite in the ordinary.

Making the Mundane Sacred

The greatest shift happens not when you meditate for hours, but when your entire life becomes a meditation.

Washing dishes, driving to work, or folding clothes — these are not distractions from your spiritual path; they are the path.

When you bring awareness into these moments, the veil between the spiritual and the physical dissolves.

The act of breathing becomes prayer.

The act of listening becomes communion.

The act of living becomes creation.

You begin to realise that every moment is an opportunity to anchor love — to infuse the world with light through presence alone.

Ascension is not a destination beyond this world.

It is the awakening of Heaven within it.

The Frequency of Gratitude

Gratitude is the golden thread that weaves spirit into form.

It is the vibration of acknowledgment — the Universe recognising itself through you.

When you wake each morning with gratitude, you align with abundance before a single event unfolds.

You remind your cells that life is a gift, not a problem to be solved.

Gratitude turns ordinary air into starlight.

Begin each day by naming three things — small or grand — that your heart appreciates.

Then breathe them into your being.

You will notice how even the challenges begin to shimmer with purpose.

Through gratitude, the frequency of your entire field lifts.

It is the simplest and most potent act of ascension available in every breath.

Walking in Light

As your energy expands and stabilises, you begin to walk differently — softer, slower, more aware of the ripples your presence creates.

Every step becomes a blessing, every interaction an exchange of frequency.

This is what it means to walk as a lightkeeper upon the Earth.

You do not need to preach, convert, or convince; your very vibration does the work.

Your smile is a transmission.

Your kindness, an activation.

Your stillness, a reminder to others of their own peace.

Living this way transforms the collective from the inside out — one radiant human at a time.

Balancing the Celestial and the Human

There will be days when the density of the world feels heavy — when old fears or shadows re-emerge.

Do not see this as failure.

It is integration.

Light reveals what is ready to be healed.

Each wave of emotion, each human challenge, is an invitation to bring love where it was once absent.

Breathe.

Return to the heart.

Ask, "How can I bring light into this moment?"

The answer will always be simple — through presence, compassion, and truth.

Remember: even the stars have nights of eclipse before shining brighter again.

Practice: Ascension in Action

1. **Morning Alignment** — Before you rise, place your hand on your heart and whisper: *"I begin this day as light in motion. Everything I touch becomes sacred."*
2. **Mindful Moments** — Throughout the day, pause often. Breathe consciously.
   Feel the world around you — the wind, the warmth, the heartbeat of life.
3. **Evening Gratitude** — Before sleep, recall three moments that felt beautiful, no matter how small.
   Thank them, release them, and let their frequency cradle you into rest.

Becoming the Living Meditation

When every breath is sacred, there is no longer a divide between your practice and your life.

You become the bridge — the embodied ascension, the living meditation.

Your light nourishes the Earth with every heartbeat.

You begin to see yourself not as a seeker of enlightenment, but as the expression of it.

This is ascension — not rising away from the world, but rising within it.

Not abandoning the human story, but turning it into poetry.

"Ascension is not about leaving Earth — it is about falling so deeply in love with it that you illuminate every inch of it with your light."

The Return to the Stars

There comes a moment in every journey of remembrance when you realise — you were never trying to reach the stars.

You were always made of them.

Your meditations, your breaths, your awakenings — they were not paths toward the divine, but doorways back into it.

Every still moment was a spark returning home.

Every quiet heartbeat, a signal beaming across the galaxies, whispering: *I remember.*

And now, beloved soul, you do.

The Great Remembering

The Return to the Stars is not an ascension upward — it is a deepening inward.

It is the realisation that the vast expanse of the cosmos has always lived inside you.

The constellations are mapped in your DNA.

The nebulae breathe in your lungs.

The Milky Way curves along the rhythm of your spine.

When you close your eyes in meditation, you do not leave Earth — you expand beyond it.

You dissolve into the field of light from which all things were born.

You become part of the cosmic dance once more — creator and creation, star and soul, one luminous breath.

This is the great return — not to a place, but to a knowing.

The Galactic Heartbeat

Every star in the Universe pulses with a rhythm — a sacred heartbeat that echoes through every atom of existence.

When your consciousness aligns with that rhythm through stillness, you feel it as peace, as love, as home.

This is the heartbeat of Source, the eternal song of Oneness.

It is what calls you in the quiet hours of night, what pulls you toward meditation, what awakens the tears that feel like remembering.

You are that pulse.

You are that song.

You are the heartbeat of the Universe learning to recognise itself again.

The Journey Was Always Within

You have travelled far, through dimensions of thought, through galaxies of emotion, through lifetimes of forgetting.

And yet, every path led back here — to your breath, to your light, to the still, sacred space inside your heart.

You came to Earth not to escape the stars, but to embody them — to bring heaven into matter, to let the cosmos feel what it means to love, to laugh, to create, to heal.

Your human life is not a limitation of your light.

It is the masterpiece through which your light expresses itself.

The Light You Leave Behind

Each time you meditate, you leave trails of starlight across the collective consciousness of humanity.

Each act of kindness, each moment of peace, sends ripples of remembrance through the grid of Earth.

You are not just changing your life — you are reawakening the frequency of a planet.

Through you, galaxies learn compassion.

Through you, the Universe evolves.

Through you, the stars remember their own light reflected in human eyes.

This is your legacy — to walk the Earth as a living constellation, to let your love become a pathway home for others still wandering.

Meditation Practice: The Homecoming

1. **Find Stillness.**
   Sit or lie down, eyes closed. Take three deep breaths, releasing all effort.
2. **Visualise.**
   See yourself standing beneath a vast night sky. The stars above shimmer like living jewels.
3. **Connect.**
   As you breathe, feel the light of the stars descending through your crown, filling your body with radiant silver and gold.

Feel the light of the Earth rising to meet it.
4. **Affirm:**
   *"I am one with the stars. I am one with the Earth.
   I am light, remembering itself."*
5. **Rest in Silence.**
   Stay here, floating between heaven and earth, between past and infinite.
   Let peace expand until there is no separation, no self — only light.

The Eternal Circle

And so, the journey comes full circle — from stillness, to awakening, to embodiment, to remembrance.

The stars you once gazed upon are now within you, shining through your every breath, your every smile, your every heartbeat.

You are the bridge between galaxies and gardens, a messenger of light walking in form.

And when your soul looks once more to the sky, it will not be with longing — but with recognition.

For you will know, with the quiet certainty of eternity itself: *You have always been home.*

"You are not a human reaching for the stars — you are a star remembering what it means to be human."

Practices for Returning Home to the Stars

1) Beyond Thought: The Sky Behind the Clouds

Thinking is a spark—restless, reactive, often scattered by whatever the world throws at it.

Meditation is the sky—vast, untroubled, always there.

As your practice deepens, you begin to notice a gentle truth: you are not your thoughts. You are the awareness witnessing them. You can choose which thoughts to follow and which to release. This is where spiritual growth blossoms, because a new question naturally arises: *If I am watching the mind… who is the watcher?*

The watcher is your luminous awareness—your star-self—quiet, expansive, eternally present.

2) Concentration & Stillness: Two Wings, One Flight

Concentration is how we enter the temple; stillness is what we find inside.

- **Concentration** gathers scattered attention—on a sound, a mantra, a candle flame, the breath.

- **Stillness** arrives when effort dissolves and awareness rests in itself—silent, spacious, whole.

Some days you'll need the focus of concentration; other days you'll fall naturally into the ocean of silence. Both are sacred.

3) How Long to Meditate (Your Rhythm of Light)

Begin gently. Five to ten minutes can be powerful. With practice, many find 15–20 minutes once or twice daily balances mind, body, and light body beautifully. Seasoned meditators may rest in silence for 20–60 minutes.

Your rule of stars: consistent and kind. Even brief, sincere practice shifts your frequency. Let duration follow devotion, not pressure.

4) Soundscapes for the Soul (Music in Meditation)

Music can open gates—masking outer noise and inviting inner harmony.

- Choose sound that feels uplifting, soothing, or trance-evoking (oceanic drones, crystal bowls, gentle ambient, soft drum journeys).
- Lyrics are fine if they are positive and don't pull you into story.
- Avoid personally triggering music or chaotic rhythms that agitate your system.

Remember: different days, different doors—silence one day, star-drumming the next.

5) When to Meditate (Celestial Timing)

Any time is sacred. Two helpful anchors:

- **Morning**: set your field for the day—clarity, ease, and cosmic coherence.
- **Midday/Evening**: create a luminous pause—clear the density of the day and reset your energy.

Meditate before meals when possible, and choose times that fit your life. The best practice is the one you'll keep.

6) Gentle Guidelines (Not Rules)

1. **Daily rhythm**: short sessions sprinkled through the day or one/two longer sits—whatever integrates gracefully.
2. **Before food**: a calmer body allows a clearer field.
3. **Choose a space**: returning to the same nook builds a conditioned doorway into calm.
4. **Aligned posture**: seated or lying down—spine long, body comfortable, breath unforced.
5. **Make it yours**: style, place, time—crafted for your soul, not someone else's routine.

7) Creating Your Star Sanctuary (Meditation Space)

Curate with the senses:

- **Sight**: soft light; candle or star lamp; a simple altar with a crystal, feather, shell, or galaxy print.
- **Sound**: gentle music, chimes, or the hush of night.
- **Scent**: a drop of lavender, sandalwood, or frankincense; fresh flowers; ocean breeze through a window.
- **Touch**: cushions, a warm throw, textures that invite relaxation.
- **Taste (your taste!)**: beauty that delights you—objects that whisper "welcome home."

Your sanctuary can be a corner of a room, a garden seat, or a repurposed cubby—privacy and peace matter more than size.

8) How Do I Meditate? (Simple Doors In)

- Sit or lie with the spine long.
- Choose a focus (breath, sound, flame, mantra, body sensation).
- When the mind wanders (it will), gently return.
- If you itch, scratch with kindness and come back.
- Let presence be tender, not stern.

9) Meditation Styles (Find Your Doorway)

A) Movement Meditation — *Starlight in Motion*

Walking: Step in the NOW. Notice sky, breeze, colour, birdsong. Walk with gratitude or a soft mantra.

Dance: At home, press play and let your body become constellation. Lose yourself in rhythm—presence through movement.

Movement clears density and trains your nervous system to choose calm under motion.

B) Zen Presence — *The Sacred Now*

Zen is simple: just this moment.

Listen to sounds, feel the breath, notice sensations. No story, no fixing—only what is. Practice anywhere—shower, queue, commute. Over time, being present becomes your brain's favourite habit.

Zen Shower: Attend to water, warmth, scent, sound. Return gently whenever the mind leaves.

Sitting Zen: Sit, breathe, listen. If thoughts appear, bow to them inwardly and return.

C) Mantra Meditation — *Words as Light Codes*

Choose a phrase that calms and expands:

"I am light, I am home." "Peace within, peace around." Repeat softly. Let the vibration do the work.

D) Creative Visualisation — *Visioning the Inner Cosmos*

Guided journeys (live or recorded) lead the mind into healing landscapes: star-gardens, crystalline temples, moonlit oceans. Ideal for visual souls.

If you're not visual: use memory and senses. Recall a place you love—the scent, temperature, sounds, textures. Or gaze at a photo/mandala (concentrative focus) and imagine stepping inside.

E) Deep Muscle Relaxation — *De-Tension, Re-Tune*

Scan from toes to crown: gently tense then release each muscle group (avoid injured areas). This trains the brain to recognise and soften tension and is a powerful pre-meditation reset.

10) When Unpleasant Sensations Arise (Alchemy of Release)

Shaking, tears, nausea, tightness, rising sadness—these can appear as the body lets go of long-held chemistry and emotion.

Think of it as density leaving your field.

Be kind: change posture, soften the breath, try a gentler style, shorten the session, or add grounding (touch the earth, sip water). If themes repeat, journal or seek supportive guidance. Return to now: in this breath, you are safe.

11) Gratitude Practice — *Rewiring for Light*

Gratitude is cosmic software for the heart. Keep a Gratitude Journal: each day list a few real, present-moment blessings. When your "emotional barometer" dips, revisit the list or speak a few new gratitudes aloud. This shifts attention from fear to possibility and stabilises your frequency in the field of abundance.

12) Affirmations — *Programming the Subconscious with Love*

Affirmations are loving instructions from your conscious mind to your ancient, protective mind.

- Speak aloud, rhythmically, often.
- Post them where you'll see them (mirror, kettle, car visor).
- Make them present-tense, kind, and believable.

Examples:

"I am calm, clear, and connected."

"I am loved, loving, and lovable."

"My body rests in safety; my light expands with ease."

Use them within meditation as mantra, or during "auto-pilot" tasks to keep your inner dialogue luminous.

13) Everyday Ways to Ease Overload (Living Lightly)

- Wake 15 minutes earlier for breath and quiet.
- Prepare simple things the night before; keep a kind list (not a whip).
- Practice *sacred no's*; ask for help sooner.
- Choose clothing that feels good on the skin.
- Touch the Earth daily; notice one wild, living thing.
- Smile at strangers; make something by hand.
- Drink more water; stretch; breathe; move.
- Write affirmations on the mirror; declutter one small space.
- Reduce stimulants when you can; add a little more sleep.
- Let others carry what is theirs; lovingly carry your own.
- Keep seeking bright ways to be well—and remember how awesome you are.

14) A Note on Learning Styles (Your Doorway, Your Way)

Visual, auditory, kinaesthetic—your soul has a native language. Choose meditation styles that speak it. If one doorway feels closed, simply try another. There is no wrong way to arrive at yourself.

15) Coming Home

Meditation is not escape. It is embodiment.

Each time you sit, breathe, walk, or dance in presence, you stitch starlight into the fabric of your day.

You are not trying to become something new— you are remembering what you have always been: a radiant being of galactic light, fully here, fully now, fully home.

The Light Remains

As you close this book, take a gentle breath and feel how far you've travelled — not in distance, but in depth.

You began with curiosity, perhaps a longing for peace or a whisper from the stars.

And now, somewhere between the stillness and the starlight, you have begun to remember who you are.

Meditation is not an escape. It is a return — to the quiet truth beneath all sound, to the infinite light beneath all form.

You have learned that you do not need to reach for the cosmos — for the cosmos already lives within your breath, your pulse, your being.

Each time you close your eyes, you touch eternity.

Each time you breathe consciously, you draw heaven into the world.

You are part of something vast and luminous — a constellation of souls awakening together, remembering that love was never lost, only forgotten for a while.

And now, you are one of the lights that helps others remember too.

So as you walk forward — into your life, into your purpose, into your next breath — do so gently, with awareness.

Let meditation be your compass, your anchor, your song.

Let love be your frequency.

Because the stars are watching, always — not from above, but from within.

They shine through your eyes when you smile.

They hum through your heart when you forgive.

They rise every time you choose peace over fear.

You are not the student of light anymore.

You are its expression.

The lesson is complete — but the light remains.

"When all else fades, remember this — the light was never out there; it was always inside of you."

Author's Note - From My Heart to Yours

This book was written as a guide, a remembrance, and a love letter — to all who have ever looked up at the night sky and felt something stir in their soul.

You are not imagining that connection.

You are remembering it.

I wrote these pages not to teach you something new, but to help you remember what you already know: that you are infinite, radiant, and divine.

That your breath is sacred.

That your stillness is powerful.

That your love is the most advanced technology the Universe has ever created.

If this journey has opened even one small door within you — a door that leads to peace, to self-trust, to wonder — then my purpose here is fulfilled.

May you continue to walk gently between worlds, grounded in this Earth yet glowing with the light of the stars.

May you meditate not only in silence, but in laughter, in gratitude, and in every heartbeat that reminds you that you are alive.

And when you forget — as we all do sometimes — look up.

The stars will remind you of what you carry within.

With infinite love and gratitude,

Mal Stevens x
Child of the Stars, Keeper of the Light, and forever a student of the Breath.

"The stars you seek in the sky are reflections of the light you have always carried within.

Acknowledgments

Thank you Marinda, Aimee, Steven, and Lily x
My Hearts and Souls. You are the true LOVES of my life.

ABOUT THE AUTHOR

MAL STEVENS - THE AUTHOR was born in the small, country town of Geraldton, Western Australia, and at the very tender age of three - after discovering a love for reading whilst sitting at her Pops feet whilst he read in his library, decided that she would someday become an Author. Often her family and friends thought her weird because no matter where she was, she could always be found with her nose in a book…and if her nose wasn't in a book because of reading it, then it could be found in one of her many hundreds of journal notebooks filled with fanciful made-up stories, and vivid descriptions about her life in general, and poetry.

Today, I am a Registered Nurse by Trade, a Mum 24/7, a Mining and Construction Industry Site Medic by day, and a writer by night. I find writing very therapeutic, and I happily and passionately lose myself to it on a daily basis.

Shine, Shine, Shine. With Lots of Love xxx

www.ingramcontent.com/pod-product-compliance
Lightning Source LLC
Chambersburg PA
CBHW022015290426
44109CB00015B/1180